IVERSIZE   COPY 20

792.092 Fehl, Fred.
F   Stars of the Broadway stage, 1940-
        1967 : in performance photographs / by
        Fred Fehl. -- New York : Dover Publica-
        tions, 1983.
            122 p. : ill. ; 31 cm.

            ISBN 0-486-24398-2 (bnd   ) : 11.45

        1.Theater--New York (N.Y.)--Pictorial
        works. 2.Actors--New York (N.Y.)--Por-
        traits.
                                            21417
                        APR 10 1984
                             D83 82-9775
        CATALOG CARD CORPORATION OF AMERICA ®   AACR2   MARC

Kim Stanley and Helen Hayes in *A Touch of the Poet,* 1958.

STARS
of the
BROADWAY STAGE
1940-1967

in Performance Photographs by
FRED FEHL

Dover Publications, Inc., New York

Copyright © 1983 by Fred Fehl.
All rights reserved under Pan American and International Copyright Conventions.

Published in Canada by General Publishing Company, Ltd., 30 Lesmill Road, Don Mills, Toronto, Ontario.
Published in the United Kingdom by Constable and Company, Ltd., 10 Orange Street, London WC2H 7EG.

Stars of the Broadway Stage, 1940–1967, in Performance Photographs by Fred Fehl is a new work, first published by Dover Publications, Inc., in 1983.

Manufactured in the United States of America
Dover Publications, Inc., 180 Varick Street, New York, N.Y. 10014

Library of Congress Cataloging in Publication Data

Fehl, Fred.
  Stars of the Broadway stage, 1940–1967, in performance photographs.

  1.Theater—New York (New York)—Pictorial works. 2. Actors—New York (New York)—Portraits. I. Title.
PN2277.N5F43 1982   792′.028′0922   82-9775
ISBN 0-486-24398-2   AACR2

Fred Fehl. (*Photo by Hans Geiger*)

Preface

I was born and raised in Vienna; from my early teens I have been interested in theater, opera and classical music. In the 1920s and 1930s I had the opportunity to see great all-star performances at the Burgtheater and at Max Reinhardt's theater in my native city.

When I came to America in 1939 after fleeing Vienna, I combined two hobbies, theater and photography, and became a theatrical photographer. I had always found studio photographs very static and I experimented with photographing during performance or dress rehearsal. I succeeded and my photographs have been greatly acclaimed and used in hundreds of magazines, newspapers and books during the past forty years.

I always maintain that only a performance offers flow of movement (especially important in dance) as well the artist's highest emotional expression. After I photographed Charles Boyer during a performance of *Red Gloves* he said that he liked my kind of pictures much better than any he had had taken in Hollywood studios. The same opinion was expressed by Marcel Marceau, who said: "It is difficult for me to pose in a studio, but your performance photographs are alive."

From 1940 to 1970 I photographed almost a thousand Broadway and off-Broadway performances, almost all with a 35-mm camera and available stage lighting. On some occasions, when I used multiple strobe lights during dress rehearsals, I used in addition a 2¼ x 3¼ camera.

In 1976, 450 of my photographs on theater, dance, the New York City Opera and famous classical musicians were on exhibit at the Lincoln Center Library for more than seven months under the title *Fred Fehl, Photographer of the Performing Arts.*

Pictures taken by me have appeared in over a hundred books and magazines. A book with my photographs of Erik Bruhn, *Beyond Technique*, with text by Mr. Bruhn, was published by Dance Perspectives in 1968. I collaborated with Melissa Hayden on the book *Melissa Hayden On Stage and Off*, published by Doubleday in 1963. *On Broadway*, my book with 450 photographs and text by William and Jane Stott, was published by the University of Texas Press in 1978. Two books using my photographs appeared in the fall of 1981: *The New York City Opera Sings*, published by the New York City Opera Guild (all 60 photos were mine), and *New York City Opera*, text by Martin Sokol, published by Macmillan (most of the photos—60—were mine). In the same season, Dance Horizon published my book of 250 performance photographs *Giselle and Albrecht*, with text by Doris Hering.

My wife Margaret and I celebrated our fortieth wedding anniversary in 1980. She is a pianist and teaches music and piano. She shares my interest in theater, dance and opera, and we can always be seen together at performances and rehearsals.

FRED FEHL

Technical Note

The general arrangement of the book is alphabetical by performers. When a picture shows more than one performer, a choice had naturally to be made for alphabetization; when the same performer occurred more than once, the choice for alphabetization fell on others shown in the additional picture or pictures. Moreover, extremely strict alphabetization was sometimes abandoned in the interest of better page groupings. The Alphabetical List of Actors and Actresses, located at the end of the picture section, shows at a glance exactly where any given performer is depicted anywhere in the book.

The Alphabetical List of Productions, at the very end of the volume, shows the location of all the plays and shows depicted in the book, and supplies the names of the playwrights and composers.

The captions on the picture pages give the years of the productions as well as the names of the productions and performers depicted. Wherever applicable, they also state whether the production in question was a revival and/or a non-Broadway production. When not otherwise indicated, these pictures are of the original Broadway run.

When a photograph shows only two men or only two women, the caption names the performers reading from left to right, unless otherwise indicated.

1. Brian Aherne and Celeste Holm in *She Stoops to Conquer,* 1949 revival.   **2.** Julie Andrews (center) in *My Fair Lady,* 1956. Left of her: Robert Coote and Rex Harrison. Right of her: Michael King and Cathleen Nesbitt.

3.

3. Judith Anderson and Maurice Evans in *Macbeth,* 1941 revival.   **4.** Judith Anderson (right), Marian Seldes and Alfred Ryder in *The Tower Beyond Tragedy,* 1950.

4

5. Carroll Baker in *Come on Strong,* 1962.   **6.** Lucille Ball in *Dream Girl,* a 1947 touring production.

7. Pearl Bailey in *Bless You All*, 1950. **8.** Josephine Baker in *Josephine Baker*, 1964. **9.** Tallulah Bankhead in *ANTA Album 1951*.

10

10. Ethel Barrymore and Mildred Dunnock in *The Corn Is Green*, 1940. **11.** Diana Barrymore and William Roerick in *The Land Is Bright*, 1941.

11

12. Betty Bartley and Bert Lahr in *ANTA Album 1951*. 13. James Barton in *ANTA Album 1949*. 14. Ed Begley and Arthur Kennedy in *All My Sons*, 1947.

15

15. Barbara Bel Geddes in *Cat on a Hot Tin Roof,* 1955.   **16.** Ralph Bellamy and Shirley Booth in *Tomorrow the World,* 1943.

16

17.

17. Herbert Berghof (right) and Luise Rainer in *The Lady from the Sea*, 1950 revival.
18. Elisabeth Bergner in *Amphitryon 38*, 1949 revival at the Glen Cove Summer Theater.

18.

19

21

20

19. Joan Blondell in *Copper and Brass,* 1957 (not the Broadway production). **20.** Mary Boland in *The Rivals,* 1942 revival. **21.** Ray Bolger in *All American,* 1962.

22. Shirley Booth in *A Tree Grows in Brooklyn*, 1951. **23.** Shirley Booth in *My Sister Eileen*, 1940.

22

23

24

25

24. Tom Bosley (right) and Nathaniel Frey in *Fiorello!*, 1959. **25.** Charles Boyer in *Red Gloves*. 1948.

26

26. Eddie Bracken and Eartha Kitt in *Shinbone Alley*, 1957.

27

27. Marlon Brando (right), Virginia Gilmore and Robert Simon in *Truckline Café*, 1946.
28. Richard Burton and Susan Strasberg in *Time Remembered*, 1957.

28

29. Yul Brynner in *The King and I*, 1951.

30

32

30. Betty Bruce and Ray Bolger in *Keep Off the Grass*, 1940. **31.** Art Carney and Elizabeth Ashley in *Take Her, She's Mine*, 1961. **32.** Louis Calhern and Arnold Moss in *King Lear*, 1950 revival.

31

33

34

33. Bobby Clark in *The Would-Be Gentleman*, 1946 revival. **34.** Carol Channing in *Gentlemen Prefer Blondes*, 1949.

35. Ina Claire (standing), Joan Greenwood and Claude Rains in *The Confidential Clerk,* 1954. **36.** Montgomery Clift and Judith Evelyn in *The Sea Gull,* 1954 revival.

35

36

37

37. Mady Christians and Mildred Natwick in *The Lady Who Came to Stay,* 1941.   **38.** Lee J. Cobb in *Death of a Salesman,* 1949.

38

39

39. Imogene Coca and William Archibald in the number "The Morning After of a Faun" in *Concert Varieties*, 1945. **40.** Robert Coote and Rex Harrison in *My Fair Lady*, 1956.

40

41. Claudette Colbert in *Island Fling*, 1951, at the Westport Country Playhouse. **42.** Barbara Cook in *The Music Man*, 1957. **43.** Hume Cronyn and Jessica Tandy in *The Man in the Dog Suit*, 1957.

44

44. Katharine Cornell (right) and Marian Seldes in *That Lady*, 1949. **45.** Alexandra Danilova and Tony Randall in *Oh Captain!*, 1958.

45

46. Sammy Davis, Jr. in *The Desperate Hours*, 1962 revival at the Westport Country Playhouse **47.** Sammy Davis, Jr., Will Mastin (left) and Sammy Davis, Sr. in *Mr. Wonderful*, 1956.

46

47

48. James Dean (right) and Arthur Kennedy in *See the Jaguar*, 1952.

49

50

51

49. Brandon de Wilde and Helen Hayes in *Mrs. McThing*, 1952.
50. Olive Deering and Paul Muni in *Counsellor-at-Law*, 1942 revival.
51. Albert Dekker (at table), Paul Scofield, Olga Bellin and Carol Goodner in *A Man for All Seasons*, 1961. **52.** Melvyn Douglas in *The Gang's All Here*, 1959. **53.** Alfred Drake in *Kismet*, 1953.

54

54. Patty Duke (right) and Anne Bancroft in *The Miracle Worker,* 1959.

55

57

56

55. Katherine Dunham and Dooley Wilson in *Cabin in the Sky*, 1940.
56. Mildred Dunnock (right) and Pearl Lang in *Peer Gynt*, 1951 revival.
57. Jimmy Durante and Ilka Chase in *Keep Off the Grass*, 1940.

58. Faye Emerson in *The Lady Chooses* (not a Broadway production) **59.** Judith Evelyn and José Ferrer in *The Shrike*, 1952. **60.** Maurice Evans and Joseph Schildkraut in *Hamlet*, 1953 television revival.

59

58

60

61

61. Wilbur Evans and Shirley Booth in *By the Beautiful Sea*, 1954.　**62.** Tom Ewell and Nancy Olson in *Tunnel of Love*, 1957.

62

63

64

63. Nanette Fabray in *Mr. President,* 1962.   **64.** Gracie Fields in *ANTA Album 1949.*

65

65. José Ferrer in *Charley's Aunt,* 1940 revival.   **66.** José Ferrer in a scene from *Cyrano de Bergerac* in *ANTA Album 1949.*

66

67

67. Geraldine Fitzgerald in *Build with One Hand* (not a Broadway production).

68

69

68. Jane Fonda in *No Concern of Mine*, 1960, Westport Country Playhouse. **69.** Arlene Francis and Melvyn Douglas in *The Little Blue Light*, 1951.

70

70. Frederic Franklin in *Song of Norway*,
1944. **71.** Helen Gallagher and John Brascia
in *Hazel Flagg*, 1953.

71

72

72. John Garfield in *Heavenly Express,*1940.
73. John Garfield and Karl Malden in *Peer Gynt,* 1951 revival.

73

74

75

74. Betty Garrett in *Call Me Mister*, 1946. **75.** William Gaxton (right) and Victor Moore in a scene from *Of Thee I Sing* in *ANTA Album 1951.* **76.** Gladys George (right) and Anita Bolster in *Lady in Waiting*, 1940.

76

77

77. John Gielgud and Margaret Leighton in *Much Ado About Nothing,* 1959 revival.

78

79

80

78. Dorothy Gish in *The Man*, 1950. **79.** Lillian Gish in *Crime and Punishment*, 1947. **80.** Hermione Gingold in *From A to Z*, 1960.

81. Ruth Gordon in *A Month in the Country,* 1949 revival at Westport Country Playhouse.
82. Beatrice Grayson and John Garfield in *Golden Boy,* 1952 revival.

84

85

83. Tammy Grimes in *The Unsinkable Molly Brown*, 1960.
84. Tammy Grimes in *Look After Lulu*, 1959 revival. **85.** Ethel
Griffies and Boris Karloff in *The Shop at Sly Corner*, 1949. **86.**
Dolly Haas and John Gielgud in *Crime and Punishment*, 1947.

86

87

87. Julie Harris in *The Member of the Wedding*, 1950.

88

89

88. Julie Harris in *A Shot in the Dark*, 1961. **89.** Julie Harris and June Havoc in *The Warm Peninsula*, 1959.

90

91

90. Juanita Hall in *Flower Drum Song*, 1958.   **91.** Walter Hampden in *The Crucible*, 1953.   **92.** Rex Harrison in *The Love of Four Colonels*, 1953.

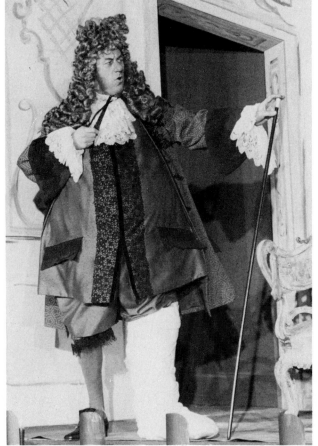

92

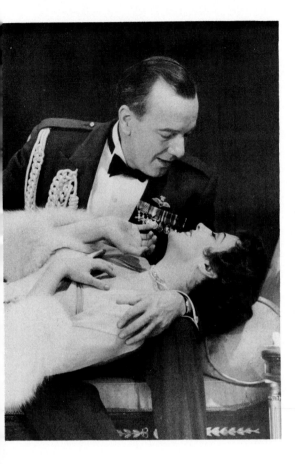

93. Rex Harrison in *Anne of the Thousand Days,* 1948.
94. Signe Hasso and Maurice Evans in *The Apple Cart,*
1956 revival.

93

96

95. June Havoc in *Pal Joey*, 1940. **96.** Helen Hayes (center) with Susan Strasberg and Sig Arno in *Time Remembered*, 1957. **97.** Eileen Heckart and Patty McCormack in *The Bad Seed*, 1954.

95

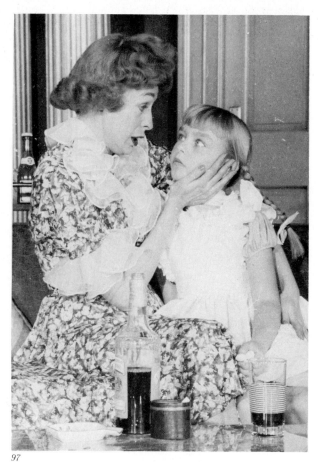

97

98

98. Francis Heflin (left), Mady Christians and Marlon Brando in *I Remember Mama,* 1944.
99. Van Heflin, Gloria Marlowe (left) and Eileen Heckart in *A View from the Bridge,* 1955.

99

100

101

100. Audrey Hepburn in *Gigi,* 1951. **101.** Judy Holliday and Peter Gennaro in *Bells Are Ringing,* 1956.

102

102. Wendy Hiller and Maurice Evans in *The Aspern Papers*, 1962. **103.** Celeste Holm, Art Smith (left) and Kevin McCarthy in *Anna Christie*, 1952 revival.

103

104

104. Oscar Homolka and Joan Tetzel in *The Master Builder*, 1955 revival.   **105.** Marsha Hunt and Alfred Drake in *Joy to the World*, 1948.

105

106

107

108

106. Josephine Hull in *The Solid Gold Cadillac,* 1953.   **107.** Martita Hunt in *The Madwoman of Chaillot,* 1948.   **108.** Hedda Hopper in *ANTA Album 1951.*

109

109. Gusti Huber, John Williams (left) and Maurice Evans in *Dial "M" for Murder,* 1952.
110. Walter Huston and Mary Wickes (left) in *The Apple of His Eye,* 1946.

110

111

111. Burl Ives and Ben Gazzara in *Cat on a Hot Tin Roof,* 1955.

112

113

112. Olga James and Sammy Davis, Jr. in *Mr. Wonderful*, 1956.
113. Oscar Karlweis and Louis Calhern in *Jacobowsky and the Colonel*,
1944. **114.** Boris Karloff in *Arsenic and Old Lace*, 1941.

114

115. Danny Kaye in *Let's Face It*, 1941.

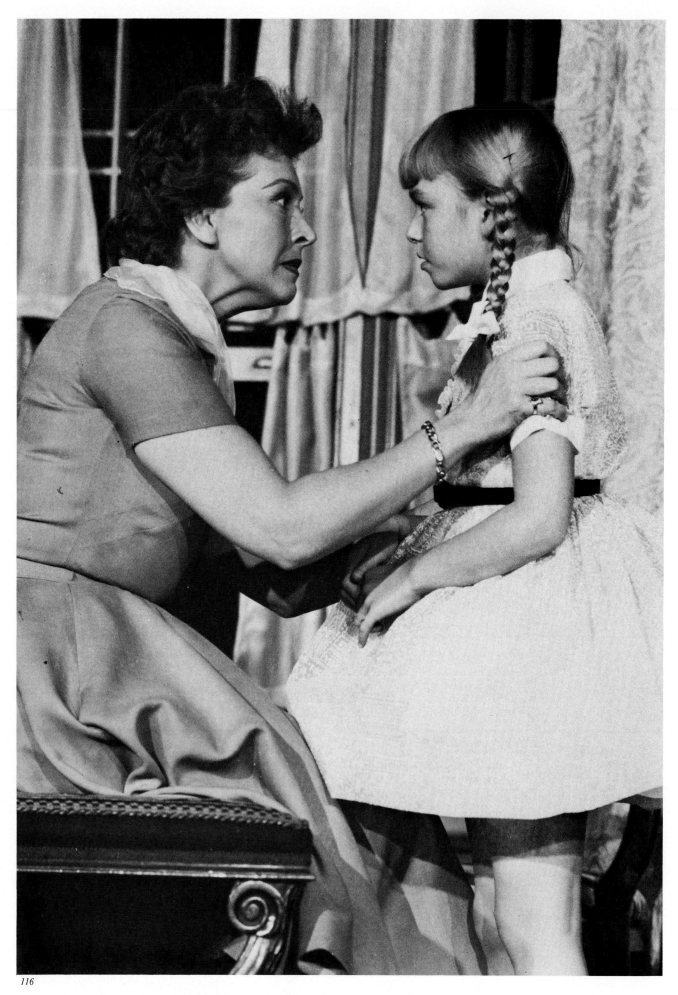

116

116. Nancy Kelly and Patty McCormack in *The Bad Seed*, 1954.

117

117. Maria Karnilova and Peter Gennaro in *By the Beautiful Sea*, 1954. **118.** Gene Kelly and Vivienne Segal in *Pal Joey*, 1940.

118

119

119. Arthur Kennedy (left), Cameron Mitchell and Lee J. Cobb in *Death of a Salesman,* 1949. **120.** John Kerr and June Havoc in *The Infernal Machine,* 1958 revival.

120

121

121. Richard Kiley in *Man of La Mancha*, 1965.

122. Richard Kiley and Gwen Verdon in *Redhead*, 1959. **123.** Larry Kert (right of center), George Marcy and Thomas Hasson (the latter two not in opening cast) in *West Side Story*, 1957.

122

123

124

125

124. Dennis King in *The Devil's Disciple*, 1950 revival. **125.** Eartha Kitt in *New Faces of 1952*.

126

126. Otto Kruger and Ralph Morgan in *The Moon Is Down*, 1942.   **127.** Bert Lahr in *Du Barry Was a Lady*, 1939 (1940 photograph).

127

128. Bert Lahr and Kathryn Mylorie in *Two on the Aisle*, 1951.

129

129. Paula Laurence and José Ferrer in *Volpone,* 1948 revival.   **130.** Gertrude Lawrence and Dennis King in *Traveller's Joy,* 1950, at the Westport Country Playhouse.

130

131

132

131. Gertrude Lawrence in *The King and I*, 1951. **132.** Gypsy Rose Lee in *Darling, Darling*, 1954, Westport Country Playhouse.

133

133. Angela Lansbury in *Anyone Can Whistle*, 1964. **134.** Charles Laughton in *Galileo*, 1947.

134

135. Vivien Leigh (right) and Mary Ure in *Duel of Angels*, 1960.

137

136. Margaret Leighton in *Separate Tables*, 1956. **137.** Beatrice Lillie in *Ziegfeld Follies*, 1957. **138.** Howard Lindsay in *One Bright Day*, 1952.

136

138

139

139. Eva Le Gallienne and Joseph Schildkraut in *Uncle Harry,* 1942.　**140.** Ella Logan and David Wayne in *Finian's Rainbow,* 1947.

140

141

141. Paul Lukas (center), Mady Christians and George Coulouris in *Watch on the Rhine*, 1941. **142.** Alfred Lunt and Lynn Fontanne in *There Shall Be No Night*, 1940.

142

143

143. Geraldine McEwan and John Gielgud in *The School for Scandal*, 1963 revival. **144.** Roddy McDowall and Andy Griffith in *No Time for Sergeants*, 1955.

144

145. Jack MacGowran (left), Melvyn Douglas and Shirley Booth in *Juno*, 1959. **146.** Myron McCormick and Mary Martin in *South Pacific*, 1949.

147

147. Marcel Marceau in *Marcel Marceau*, 1965. **148.** Aline MacMahon and John Garfield in *Heavenly Express*, 1940.

148

149

149. E. G. Marshall (left), Arthur Kennedy and Beatrice Straight in *The Crucible,* 1953.
150. Mary Martin and the children (alphabetically: Kathy Dunn, Evanna Lien, Mary Susan Locke, Lauri Peters, Marilyn Rogers, William Snowden, Joseph Stewart) in *The Sound of Music,* 1959.

150

151

152

151. Mary Martin in *The Sound of Music*, 1959. **152.** Karl Malden in *Truckline Café*, 1946.

155

154

153. Fredric March (right) and Douglas Campbell in *Gideon*, 1961. **154.** Raymond Massey (right) and Roddy McDowall in *The Tempest*, 1955 revival at Stratford, Conn. **155.** Daniel Massey and Barbara Cook in *She Loves Me*, 1963. **156.** Walter Matthau and Cedric Hardwicke in *The Burning Glass*, 1954.

156

157. Eddie Mayehoff and Cyril Ritchard in *Visit to a Small Planet*, 1957. **158.** Sanford Meisner and Melvyn Douglas in *The Bird Cage*, 1950.

159

159. Melina Mercouri and Orson Bean (seated) in *Illya Darling,* 1967.   **160.** Burgess Meredith and Ingrid Bergman in *Liliom,* 1940 revival.

160

161

161. Ethel Merman in *Annie Get Your Gun*, 1946.

162

162. Ethel Merman and Paul Lukas in *Call Me Madam*, 1950. **163.** Ethel Merman and Erv Harmon in *Gypsy*, 1959.

163

165

164

164. Patricia Morison and Alfred Drake in *Kiss Me, Kate,* 1948. **165.** Robert Morley as Oscar Wilde in *ANTA Album 1949.* **166.** Zero Mostel in *A Funny Thing Happened on the Way to the Forum,* 1962.

166

167

167. Zero Mostel (right) and Uta Hagen in *The Good Woman of Setzuan*, 1956.   **168.** Thomas Mitchell and Helen Gallagher in *Hazel Flagg*, 1953.

168

169

171

169. Arnold Moss in *The Land Is Bright*, 1941. **170.** Paul Muni (right) and Ed Begley in *Inherit the Wind*, 1955. **171.** Patricia Neal in *A Roomful of Roses*, 1955. **172.** Mildred Nat–wick in *Blithe Spirit*, 1941.

170

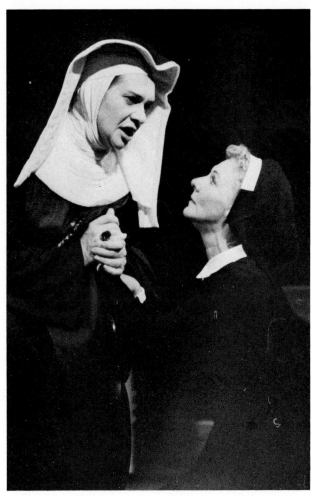

174

175

173. Cathleen Nesbitt and Audrey Hepburn in *Gigi,* 1951. **174.** Sono Osato and John Garfield in *Peer Gynt,* 1951 revival. **175.** Patricia Neway and Mary Martin in *The Sound of Music,* 1959. **176.** Elliott Nugent and Martha Scott in *The Male Animal,* 1952 revival.

176

177

177. Paul Newman and Geraldine Page in *Sweet Bird of Youth*, 1959.

178

178. Geraldine Page and Paul Newman in *Sweet Bird of Youth*, 1959.

179

179. Maureen O'Sullivan and Paul Ford in *Never Too Late,* 1962.   **180.** Jack Palance (right) and Claude Rains in *Darkness at Noon,* 1951.

180

181

181. Gregory Peck in *Sons and Soldiers*, 1943. 182. Alice Pearce and Tom Ewell in *Small Wonder*, 1948. 183. Lilli Palmer in *The Love of Four Colonels*, 1953.

182

183

184

185

184. Molly Picon in *Milk and Honey,* 1961.   **185.** Irra Pettina in *Candide,* 1956.   **186.** Anthony Perkins in *Greenwillow,* 1960.   **187.** Ezio Pinza and Mary Martin in *South Pacific,* 1949.   **188.** Eric Portman and Kim Stanley in *A Touch of the Poet,* 1958.

186   188

187

189

189. Robert Preston and Barbara Cook in *The Music Man*, 1957.   **190.** Tyrone Power and Leora Dana in *A Quiet Place*, 1955 (photographed in New Haven; closed before N.Y.).

190

191. Anthony Quayle and Eileen Herlie in *Halfway Up the Tree*, 1967.

193

194

192. Luise Rainer in *Joan of Lorraine*, 1947 (not on Broadway). **193.** John Raitt and Carol Haney in *The Pajama Game*, 1954. **194.** Lee Remick and Harry Guardino in *Anyone Can Whistle*, 1964.

195

196

195. Claude Rains and Christopher Plummer in *The Night of the Auk*, 1956.
196. Vincent Price and Judith Evelyn in *Angel Street*, 1941.

198

197. Ralph Richardson in *The School for Scandal*, 1963 revival. **198.** Michael Redgrave in *The Sleeping Prince*, 1956.

197

199

199. Cyril Ritchard (left), David Wayne and Glynis Johns in *Too True to Be Good*, 1963 revival. **200.** Jason Robards, Jr. and Hume Cronyn in *Big Fish, Little Fish*, 1961.

200

201

202

201. Edward G. Robinson (left) and Leon Gordon in the road company of *Darkness at Noon*, 1961.   **202.** Chita Rivera and Ken Le Roy in *West Side Story*, 1957.

203

203. Bill Robinson in *All in Fun*, 1940.   **204.** Flora Robson in *Ladies in Retirement*, 1940.

204

205

205. Jimmy Savo in *What's Up*, 1943.   **206.** Polly Rowles (center), Nancy Malone and Melvyn Douglas in *Time Out for Ginger*, 1952.

206

207

209

207. Robert Ryan in *Coriolanus*, 1954 revival. **208.** Paul Scofield in *A Man for All Seasons*, 1961. **209.** Fritzi Scheff in *ANTA Album 1950*.

208

210

210. Joseph Schildkraut and Susan Strasberg in *The Diary of Anne Frank*, 1955. **211.** Menasha Skulnik and Richard Whorf in *The Fifth Season*, 1953. **212.** George C. Scott and Marian Seldes in *The Wall*, 1960.

211

212

213

213. Marian Seldes and Judith Anderson in *The Tower Beyond Tragedy*, 1950.

214

215

214. Kim Stanley in *Bus Stop*, 1955. **215.** Muriel Smith and Luther Saxon in *Carmen Jones*, 1943. **216.** Albert Sharpe and Ella Logan in *Finian's Rainbow*, 1947.

216

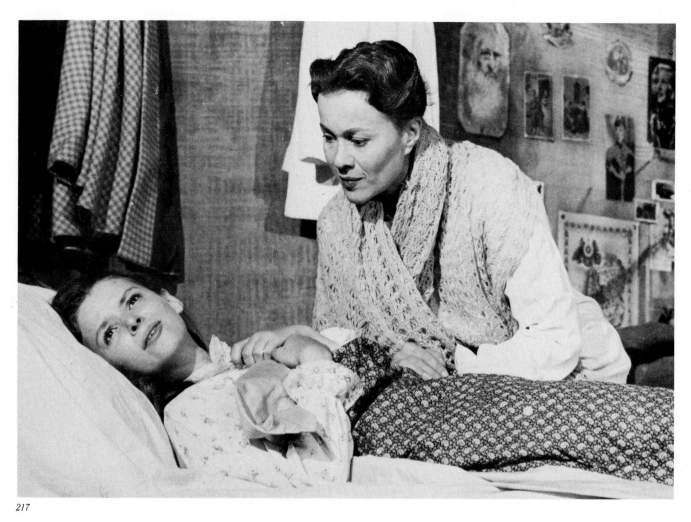

217

217. Susan Strasberg (on bed) and Gusti Huber in *The Diary of Anne Frank*, 1955. **218.** Margaret Sullavan and Elliott Nugent in *The Voice of the Turtle*, 1943.

218

219

219. Elaine Stritch in *Bus Stop*, 1955. **220.** Maureen Stapleton in *The Cold Wind and the Warm*, 1958. **221.** William Tabbert and Juanita Hall in *South Pacific*, 1949.

220

221

222

222. Lyle Talbot and Glenda Farrell in *Separate Rooms*, 1940. **223.** Richard Thomas (standing) and Christopher Norris (on bed) in *The Playroom*, 1965.

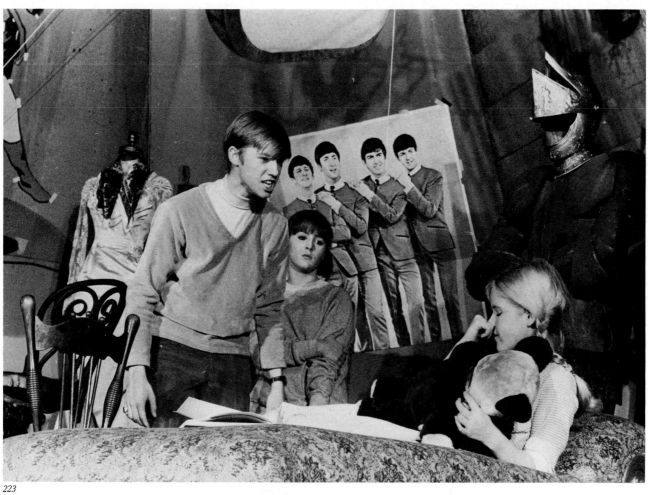

223

224

225

227

224. Torın Thatcher, Patty Duke and Patricia Neal in *The Miracle Worker*, 1959. **225.** Franchot Tone and Brooke Hayward in *Mandingo*, 1961. **226.** Constance Towers and Lillian Gish in *Anya*, 1965. **227.** Helen Traubel in *Pipe Dream*, 1955.

226

228

229

230

228. Dick Van Dyke and Chita Rivera in *Bye Bye Birdie*, 1960. **229.** Gwen Verdon in *New Girl in Town*, 1957. **230.** Gwen Verdon in *Can-Can*, 1953.

231

232

231. Nancy Walker in *Fallen Angels*, 1956 revival. **232.** Eli Wallach and Morris Carnovsky in *The Cold Wind and the Warm*, 1958.

233

233. Richard Waring and Ethel Barrymore in *The Corn Is Green*, 1940. **234.** Margaret Webster and Shepperd Strudwick in *The Three Sisters*, 1950 revival at the Woodstock Playhouse.

234

236

235. Clifton Webb in *Blithe Spirit*, 1941. **236.** Peggy Wood in *Blithe Spirit*, 1941.

235

237

237. Emlyn Williams (left) and Jeremy Brett (right) in *The Deputy*, 1964.

238

239

238. Ethel Waters and Dooley Wilson in *Cabin in the Sky,*
1940. **239.** Vera Zorina and Nicolas Orloff in *On Your Toes,* 1954 revival.

240

240. David Wayne (center) and John Forsythe in *Teahouse of the August Moon,* 1953.

Alphabetical List of Actors and Actresses

The numbers are those of the illustrations.

Alphabetical List of Productions

Titles beginning with "A" or "The" are listed after the word following. The numbers are those of the illustrations. The playwrights' names are given in parentheses except in the case of a few plays that did not appear on Broadway.